Does He Love Me?

Written by
Rob Waring and **Maurice Jamall**
(with contributions by **Julian Thomlinson**)

Before You Read

to cry			movie theater	
to lie			party	
birthday			rose	
café			secret	
diary			soda	
head			test	
library			stupid	

In the story

Jenny

Alex

Yoon-Hee

Gemma

"There she is!" thought Jenny. Jenny was in the school library. She was looking for her best friend, Yoon-Hee. She was very happy because she wanted to show her friend a rose.

Yoon-Hee was in the library writing in her diary. She started writing the diary when she was 8 years old. She writes everything in it. She writes all her feelings, all her ideas. She writes all her secrets.

Yoon-Hee saw Jenny. She closed the diary quickly. She did not want anybody to read it.

"Hi Jenny," she said. "How's everything?"

"Great, thanks," she said, smiling. "Yoon-Hee, this is from Alex. It's nice, isn't it?" She showed her the rose.

"Yeah. You're so lucky," said Yoon-Hee. "I hope I can have a boyfriend like Alex one day. He's so nice."

Jenny looked at Yoon-Hee's diary. "Are you writing about me today?" asked Jenny, smiling.

"Ahh . . . That's my secret!" Yoon-Hee said, smiling back. Jenny knew Yoon-Hee's diary was a secret.

"There's an important day coming soon. I hope it is in your diary," said Jenny.

"Oh," said Yoon-Hee. "What day?"

"It's okay," said Jenny. "You'll remember." But Jenny thought, "Did Yoon-Hee forget the big day?"

Jenny said, "Yoon-Hee, I'm going shopping after school today. Alex can't come. He's playing soccer. Do you want to come? It'll be fun."

"Oh, after school? Umm . . . No, thanks. I'm playing tennis. Sorry," replied Yoon-Hee.

Jenny replied, "That's okay. Maybe we can go shopping another time."

"Yes, I'd like that," replied her friend.

After school, Jenny was shopping in town with her little sister, Jessica. They were looking in all the stores. Then Jessica saw Alex. She was excited because she liked Alex. Jessica said, "Jenny, look! Is that Alex over there?"

"Where?" asked Jenny.

"There, sitting in the café with Yoon-Hee," said Jessica, pointing at him.

"Yes, it is," said Jenny. "Let's go and see him."

Jenny looked in the café. She saw Alex with Yoon-Hee. They were talking. They were sitting very close. Alex was saying something quietly to Yoon-Hee. She was smiling. They were laughing together.

"What are they talking about?" Jenny thought. "Why are they talking like that? They are a little *too* friendly," she thought. "That's strange." She went into the café to talk to them.

Alex saw Jenny come into the café. When they saw Jenny, they jumped in surprise.

"Look out! Here comes Jenny!" said Alex quietly.

They quickly moved away. Alex took some papers and put them in his bag.

"That's strange," Jenny thought. "What are they doing here together?"

Yoon-Hee and Alex looked a little worried.

"Hi!" Jenny said. "Yoon-Hee, I thought you were playing tennis."

Suddenly, Yoon-Hee said, "Umm, well . . . I . . . I . . . was . . . Well, umm . . . I'm not." Her face turned red.

Jenny was very surprised. "Is she lying to me?" she thought.
Yoon-Hee said, "Okay, I have to go now, bye." She left the café quickly.

"Umm . . . Hi, Jenny. How are you, today?" asked Alex.

Jenny asked, "Hi, Alex. I'm okay. What are you doing here?"

"I'm . . . I'm having a soda," said Alex.

Jenny replied, "But you said you were playing soccer . . ."

"Did I? No, I wanted to meet Yoon-Hee to talk about the test next week," he replied

"What test?" asked Jenny. "But we don't have any tests next week!"

"What's going on with you and Yoon-Hee, Alex?" Jenny asked.

Alex looked at her and replied, "Nothing is going on, Jenny. I'm your boyfriend. Please believe me."

Jenny smiled, "Yes, of course I believe you, Alex."

Jenny thought, "Of course. Alex is a good boyfriend. He would never lie to me."

Then she said, "Alex, *Love on the Seas* is on at the movie theater. You promised to take me. And there's a big day coming soon, remember?"

"Really? Is there?" he said. "I'm sorry, I have to study. Maybe some other day."

"That's okay," said Jenny. "Don't worry." But Jenny was worried. "Did he forget the big day, too?" she thought.

The next day in school, Jenny saw Yoon-Hee in class. She was writing something in her diary. She did not want people to see. Yoon-Hee was thinking about something.

"Hi, Yoon-Hee," said Jenny.

Suddenly, Yoon-Hee saw Jenny and she jumped. She closed the diary very quickly.

"That's strange. What's she writing about?" thought Jenny.

"Oh, umm . . . Hi, Jenny," Yoon-Hee said. "How are you?"
"Great," Jenny replied. "Yoon-Hee, do you want to go to a movie tonight? I really want to see *Love on the Seas*. I don't think Alex wants to see it."
"Tonight? Oh, I'm sorry I can't. I have to help my family," she said. "Maybe another time."
"I see," said Jenny. "That's okay." But she was sad.

Later, Jenny saw Gemma at the bus stop. Nobody liked Gemma because she loved to tell lies about people. She loved to know bad news about everybody.

"Hi, Jenny. Are you okay?" she asked.

"Yes, I think so," Jenny replied. She was thinking about Yoon-Hee and Alex.

"Well, I just saw your boyfriend go into the movie theater with Yoon-Hee," said Gemma.

Jenny replied, "No, you didn't."

"Yes, I did! They went to see *Love on the Seas*. I saw them buy tickets," she said. Gemma smiled strangely at Jenny.

"That's a lie!" Jenny said. "Alex would never do that. He's my boyfriend, not Yoon-Hee's."

"Well, go and see when they come out of the movie theater," replied Gemma. "It finishes at 7:45."

Jenny replied, "No. I won't go, you're telling lies! As usual."

"Okay, well I told you first," said Gemma, laughing. "Bye, Jenny! Ha ha ha!" Gemma walked away, laughing.

"I hate Gemma," thought Jenny. "Why does she want to make trouble for everybody?"

Later when Jenny was walking home, she walked near the movie theater. She thought about Alex. "Was Gemma right? Are Alex and Yoon-Hee really at the movies?"

She thought, "I wanted to see *Love on the Seas* with Alex. I asked him but he said no, he didn't want to see it. They can't be in there, because he's studying. And Yoon-Hee's helping her family."

She smiled as she thought about Alex. "Don't be a fool, Jenny. Gemma is lying. She just wants to hurt me because she likes Alex. He's not watching the movie with Yoon-Hee. I know my Alex."

Jenny was at home doing her homework. "I can't do this homework," she thought. "I'll call Alex, he'll know the answers." Jenny called Alex's home. His mother, Mrs. Oliveira, answered the phone.

"Hello, Mrs. Oliveira. May I speak with Alex, please?" she asked.

"Oh hello, Jenny," said Mrs. Oliveira. "I'm sorry Alex is not in."

Jenny asked, "Oh. Where is he, do you know? I need to ask him a question."

Mrs. Oliveira said, "He went to the movie theater, I think."

"A movie? Oh, okay. Thank you, Mrs. Oliveira," said Jenny.

She was worried. She thought, "Why is Alex watching a movie? He said he was studying tonight."

The next day, Jenny saw Alex. "Hi, Alex. How are you?" she asked.

"I'm great. What's up?" he said.

"Oh, nothing!" said Jenny. She was a little angry. "I called you last night. You weren't at home."

Alex replied, "Yeah, I went out."

"Oh?" said Jenny. "I wanted to go out with you last night."

"Umm . . . Yes. I . . . umm . . . just went to buy something," he replied.

"Oh, Jenny," said Alex. "Please come to the café tonight at about 6 o'clock. Don't be late!"

Jenny said, "Oh, sure, Alex. I'll see you tonight at 6."

Jenny went to the library. She was looking for her friend,
Yoon-Hee. But she was not there. Jenny saw her friend, Kerry.
"Hi, Kerry," she said. "I'm looking for Yoon-Hee. Is she here?"
"No, but she was here 5 minutes ago," said Kerry.
Jenny saw the paper about *Love on the Seas* on the table.
"What's this?" she asked.
"We were talking about the movie," Kerry replied. She gave
Jenny the paper about *Love on the Seas*. Then she said, "I must
be going now. See you later."
Jenny was shocked. "Oh, okay. See you."

She thought, "But Yoon-Hee said she had to help her family. I don't understand. Alex said he wanted to study, but he didn't. Maybe he did go to the movie with Yoon-Hee . . ." Then she had a terrible thought. "Maybe Gemma was right! Alex is now going out with Yoon-Hee! Alex loves Yoon-Hee now! He went to see *Love on the Seas* with her, not with me!" Jenny was really shocked.

"Maybe Alex is in love with Yoon-Hee now. Yoon-Hee! My best friend!"

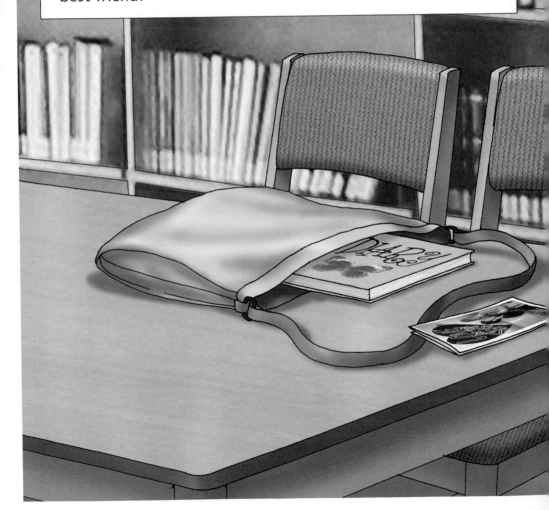

Jenny thought for a long time. She remembered that Alex and Yoon-Hee were very friendly in the café. She wanted to ask Yoon-Hee about her and Alex. But Yoon-Hee was not there. Then Jenny saw Yoon-Hee's diary in her bag.
"That's it!" she thought. "If I look in her diary, I can find out. I will know everything. Yoon-Hee writes everything in her diary. She will write about her and Alex."
She looked at the diary in Yoon-Hee's bag. And then she thought, "No, I can't read her diary, it's her secret. She's my best friend. I can't read it."
Then something in her head said "Read it! You will find out." She decided to read it.

Jenny opened the diary. She read.

June 17th
I met Alex today. We talked about Jenny.
She doesn't know. We must find a place Jenny
can't find us. We're going to meet in the café
tomorrow. I can't wait. It's going to be great.

She read some more.

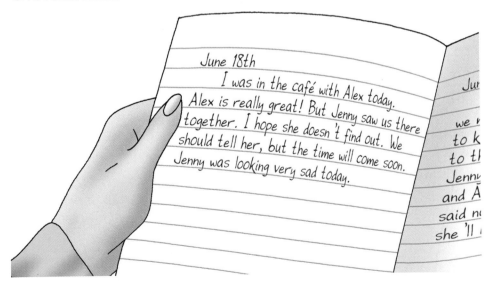

June 18th
I was in the café with Alex today.
Alex is really great! But Jenny saw us there
together. I hope she doesn't find out. We
should tell her, but the time will come soon.
Jenny was looking very sad today.

Jenny read on.

June 19th
Jenny found us in the café yesterday so we must be careful. We don't want Jenny to know what we're doing. Alex and I went to the movie theater yesterday. I think Jenny thinks something is happening with me and Alex. I wanted to tell her, but Alex said no. I feel bad for Jenny, but tomorrow she'll know.

ning.
there
We
soon.

Jenny closed the diary. "So, I'm right!" she thought. "Alex and Yoon-Hee went to the movies together. They *are* going out together. And they don't want to tell me. Oh no! My Alex!"

Jenny sat down. She put her head in her hands and she cried. "Alex. Alex. Alex! Now I know why they forgot the big day tomorrow. He's going out with my best friend! He doesn't like me any more." She cried for a long time. Jenny was very sad. But she had to go to class.

She thought, "I can see Alex in the class. I will ask him then. I want to know what's happening."

She walked slowly to class. "Does he love me?" she thought. "Oh, my Alex." She started crying again.

When Jenny went into the classroom, everybody looked at her. "They were talking about me!" she thought. "What are they talking about? What do they know?"

Then Alex came to see Jenny. "Hi, Jenny," he said. He smiled at her. It was a big, friendly smile.

Jenny was surprised. "Why is he smiling at me? He went to the movies with Yoon-Hee. I don't understand. Is he laughing at me?" she thought.

"See you tonight," he said.

Jenny thought for a long time. "I don't want Alex if he's going out with Yoon-Hee. He's not going to say goodbye to me. *I'll* say goodbye to him. But I'll do it tonight, not here in front of the others."

At 6 o'clock Jenny went to the café to meet Alex. But Alex was there with Yoon-Hee. She was very shocked. "Why's Yoon-Hee here with . . . *my* Alex?" she thought.

She said, "Alex, I want to know what's going on. Why is Yoon-Hee here?"

Alex replied, "What are you saying?"

"Last night, you said you were studying," Jenny said. "But you went to the movies with Yoon-Hee. Gemma told me. You didn't go with me! You went with her!" She pointed at Yoon-Hee. Yoon-Hee was very shocked. "And she's my best friend, too! How could you? You lied to me!" She was angry now.

"Yes, we went to the theater but . . . ," said Alex.

Jenny shouted, "So Gemma was right. You *did* go to the movies with her!"

Alex said, "Jenny, I want to say something. Please listen . . ."

Jenny was really angry with Alex. "No," she said. "I know what's happening. I'm not a fool. You listen to me."

She picked up a drink. "No, you listen to this . . ." she said. She threw some soda at Alex!

"Jenny!" said Alex. "Please! What are you thinking? What did I say? What did I do?"

Just then the door opened. Many of Jenny's friends came into the room.

"SURPRISE!!" said everybody. "Happy birthday! Happy birthday, Jenny!" they said.

Yoon-Hee said, "Jenny. We're sorry about that. We were planning this surprise party for you. We're having the party today because we have a great day planned for you and Alex, tomorrow. See?" She showed Jenny some papers.

Now Jenny understood everything. She knew that Alex was not going out with Yoon-Hee. They were planning her birthday party!

"I'm a fool," she thought. "How could I think Alex was seeing Yoon-Hee? Oh no!"

Jenny's face went very red. She ran away.

"Hey, Jenny. Come back!" shouted Alex. "Where are you going? It's your birthday party!"

But Jenny did not listen. She ran out of the café, crying.

"What's wrong with Jenny?" asked Yoon-Hee. "What happened?"

"I don't know," said Alex. "I just don't know. What did I do wrong?"

Everybody was very shocked.

Jenny was outside the café. She was still crying. "I'm a fool," she thought. "Alex was so kind to plan the surprise party for me. I didn't believe him. And I didn't believe Yoon-Hee. I looked in Yoon-Hee's diary, too." She cried more.

"And then I threw the soda in Alex's face in front of everybody!" she thought. "He'll hate me now. Why did I do that? That wasn't very smart!" she cried. Jenny was very, very sad.

Alex and Yoon-Hee looked for Jenny. They found her outside the café.

"Please don't be angry with me," said Jenny. "I . . . I didn't know about the party. I was worried. I thought you liked Yoon-Hee more than me."

Alex laughed, "Jenny, no. *You're* my girlfriend, not Yoon-Hee. We were planning the party when you saw us in the café."

He continued, "We didn't want you to know. We went to the movie theater to buy these tickets. We didn't see *Love on the Seas* together. We only bought the tickets together. You and I are going to see it after the party tonight." Alex showed Jenny the tickets.

Yoon-Hee said, "And we're having the surprise party today because we've planned a great day for you both tomorrow. You're going to have a great birthday."

Jenny was so surprised and so happy, she cried again. "So, you're not angry with me?" she asked.

"No, of course not," said Alex. "But I am wet!"

"Come back to the party, Jenny," said Yoon-Hee. "We want you to have a great birthday. And later you can go to the movie with Alex."

All she could say was, "Thank you, thank you!" And she cried again.